a passion for pastry

a passion for pastry

50 sensational recipes from britain's top chefs and food writers

edited by Roz Denny

Acknowledgements and Picture Credits:

MARY CADOGAN: Lamb and Rosemary Envelopes. This recipe first appeared in *BBC Good Food Magazine*. BARNEY DESMAZERY is Deputy Food Editor of *BBC Good Food Magazine*. JILL DUPLEIX is the Cookery Editor of *The Times*. MOYRA FRASER is Consultant Cookery Editor of *Good Housekeeping* and her portrait is by Tony Hutchings. AMANDA GRANT: Big Sausage and Apple Pastry. This recipe first appeared in *Toddler Healthy Eating Planner* published by Mitchell Beazley. LULU GRIMES: Goat's Cheese, Leek and Tapenade Parcels. This recipe first appeared in *Food Cook Eat*, published by Murdoch Books. GRACE HENDERSON of *My Weekly*: Custard Tarts, recipe courtesy of the British Egg Information Service. ALASTAIR HENDY: portrait by David Loftus. DIANA HENRY: Beef, Wild Mushroom and Claret Pie. This recipe first appeared in *House & Garden Magazine*. MARK HIX: Cinnamon Fruit Cigars. This recipe first appeared in *The Independent Magazine*. PRUE LEITH OBE: Goat's Cheese with Seasame Seeds in Filo is from *Leith's Cookery Bible* by Prue Leith and Caroline Waldegrave and the portrait of Prue Leith by Matthew Leighton Photography. SUE McMAHON is Cookery Editor of *Woman's Weekly*. ANGELA NILSEN: Moroccan Spiced Pie. This recipe first appeared in *BBC Good Food Magazine*. JAMIE OLIVER: Artichoke Pie photograph by David Loftus. SHONA CRAWFORD POOLE is Food and Drink Editor of *Country Living Magazine* and her portrait is by Sandra Lousada. RICK STEIN: Crab and Gruyère Tartlets. This recipe is from *Rick Stein's Seafood*, published by BBC Books. JOHN WILLIAMS is Executive Chef at The Ritz and Executive Chairman of the Academy of Culinary Arts.

This book first published in 2005

Designed and produced for Jus-Rol by
Grub Street
4 Rainham Close
London
SW11 6SS
Email: food@grubstreet.co.uk
Web: www.grubstreet.co.uk

Concept and compilation by Richmond Towers
Copyright this edition © Jus-Rol 2005
Recipes © Individual contributors
Home Economist for photography Philippa Vanstone
Photographs by Michelle Garrett
Photographer's Assistant Lisa Shalet
Design by AB3 Design
Printed and bound in Spain by Bookprint, S.L.

ISBN 1 904010 99 7

Contents

Foreword

Thank you for buying this book. Your reward will be many delicious treats and the knowledge that you have also helped the work of one of the country's most important food education charities.

For the past 25 years, the Academy of Culinary Arts and its leading chef, restaurant and supplier members, has been at the forefront of promoting public awareness and appreciation of the highest standards of food, cooking and service by example and education. In addition, it offers encouragement and opportunities to young people in the catering industry through guidance and training.

We do all of this through a number of education and training initiatives and the Academy's Adopt a School Trust, a charity in its own right, is one of the most important of these.

Adopt a School is a proven programme that is much in demand. It has been going for over 12 years and through it our Academicians teach primary and secondary school children about the pleasure, variety and provenance of food and how to cook, albeit to a limited extent.

The impact of our work in schools is valued and proven. The extent of Adopt a School is only limited by the amount of money we can raise for the charity.

We are delighted to be the main beneficiary of this book. On behalf of future generations of children, who will hopefully develop a passion for food (including pastry!) through the work of the Academy, our sincere thanks go to Jus-Rol for this most excellent initiative.

Happy 50th anniversary Jus-Rol and may your pastry efforts prosper for many years to come.

Brian J. Turner CBE
President
Academy of Culinary Arts

Introduction

The passion for pastry that created the birth of Jus-Rol in 1954 can be clearly traced to a time when the British were getting on their feet again after the hardships of a world war.

The 1950s saw an explosion in the wider availability of different types of foods – and foods in more convenient forms - as well as in the ownership of fridges and freezers.

Although the first use of the term 'puff pastry' seems to have been in an Italian-English dictionary of 1598, it was not until 1954 that the recipes that made a virtue of this light, crisp and delicate pastry could be enjoyed by all.

Frozen puff pastry was the first product to be sold under the Jus-Rol name in 1954. It was an instant hit not least because it came ready to roll and delivered perfect results every time.

Over the past 50 years, the Jus-Rol name has become synonymous with perfect baking results and has become a much loved food brand with every type of cook and chef.

We are passionate about our pastry and equally passionate about encouraging future generations to enjoy and appreciate good food and the pleasures of cooking as much as we do.

This is why we applaud the efforts of the Academy of Culinary Arts and its Adopt a School Trust.

The creation of this book on the occasion of Jus-Rol's 50th Anniversary is to support the future work of Adopt a School. Through the generous contributions of some of the biggest and best names in the world of food, we have hopefully created a collection of outstanding recipes that will inspire and delight.

I could not have hoped for a more positive and generous response from each and every one of the contributors. Our sincere thanks go to all of them.

Thanks also go to Roz Denny who has diligently edited the book, to Anne Dolamore of publishers Grub Street for ensuring that we have the best looking pastry book of all time, to Michelle Garrett for her yummy photographs and the Richmond Towers team who came up with the idea in the first place and have made sure everything that did have to happen has happened.

Finally, thank you for buying this book and in so doing supporting our fundraising efforts. I know you will enjoy it.

Alan McClure
Commercial Manager, Jus-Rol

Baking Basics

Making the most of ready-made pastry

First, ensure frozen pastry is well thawed before use. Follow pack instructions for timings as room temperatures vary.

- To stop the pastry sticking, lightly dust the work surface and rolling pin with flour – not too much, just little flicks.

- Hold the pin at both ends and press lightly down on the pin as you roll. Too heavy a hand will stretch the pastry and make it tough.

- Roll out pastry away from you, giving a quarter turn every three or four strokes. If necessary, slide a palette knife under it to loosen.

- For round shapes give a quarter turn after each roll.

- To line a tart or flan case, roll out the pastry to a good 5cm larger than the tin (counting in the sides as well as the diameter). So a 20cm flan tin with 2cm sides will need a 29-30cm round. Carefully lift up the pastry over the rolling pin and gently unroll over the tin.

- Take care not to stretch pastry when lifting it.

- Using your fingertips, ease the pastry down against the sides of the tin, pressing well into the base all round. To remove excess pastry, roll the pin across the top of the tin to cut off dough then using your thumb and forefinger gently press the pastry up the sides of the tin, to stand slightly proud of the top. This helps compensate for any shrinkage during cooking.

- Always allow pastry to relax after rolling and before baking. 15-20 minutes is ample, generally whilst the oven is preheating.

- Place the flan tin or dish on a metal baking dish during baking to help the pastry base cook evenly, especially when baking blind. (see opposite.)

- Use a sharp knife when trimming edges so it doesn't tear the pastry. This also helps puff pastry edges rise in neat layers.

- If covering a pie with pastry, make sure the filling is cold before you cover it. Uncooked pastry placed on hot fillings becomes soggy and can bake tough.

Re-rolling pastry trimmings

For shortcrust pastry, simply knead leftover dough gently into a smooth ball then roll as before.

For puff pastry, stack the trimmings on top of each other to keep the layers.

Knocking up pie edges

If you want to make a traditional rimmed pie, first roll out and cut out pastry slightly larger than the top of the pie dish. Re-roll the trimmings to long strips about 1.5cm wide. Press these on the edge of the pie dish.

Spoon the cooled filling into the dish. Brush the pastry edge with egg and lift the pastry pie top over it, pressing down on the eggy edge to seal. Using the back of a knife, chop lightly several times into the pastry edge whilst you press down on the edge with the back of your forefinger. This is known as 'knocking up' and helps to give added rise to the rim.

Then you can press your index finger down on the rim and cut into it with the back of a knife for a scalloped effect.

Filo pastry

Comes ready rolled and is layered up, brushed in between with melted butter, ghee (for an aromatic flavour) or olive oil. Jus-Rol filo pastry requires slightly less melted fat or oil than other brands. Instead of cutting overhanging filo, simply scrunch it on top for an attractive finish. Do keep unused filo sheets covered with cling film to stop them drying out and wrap any leftovers well to keep them moist.

Glazing

- For a shiny golden glaze, beat a whole egg thoroughly. For a professional chef's glaze, beat an egg yolk with 1-2 teaspoons of cold water. Milk can be used for a more economical glaze.

- Sweet pies made with shortcrust or sweet dessert pastry can be brushed lightly with cold water and dredged with caster sugar just before the end of the cooking time. Sweet pies made with puff pastry are best glazed with egg white and sugar before baking.

- Continental patisserie recipes are glazed by sprinkling liberally with icing sugar after cooking then returned to the oven for 8-10 minutes to caramelise the sugar.

- Filo pastry is nice glazed with melted butter, ghee or oil.

Baking blind

After filling the flan tin or dish with pastry, trim the top allowing a little to peek above the rim. Prick the base and fill with a large round of non-stick baking parchment or foil and ceramic or dried baking beans. Chill for 20 minutes whilst you heat the oven to the recommended temperature, generally 200°C, Gas 6.

Place the flan case on a metal baking sheet and bake blind for about 15 minutes, then remove the paper and beans and return the flan to the oven for another 5 minutes until the base no longer looks raw. Remove and cool.

Janet Bishop
Jus-Rol Home Economist

Asparagus and Mushroom Pastries

ANTONY WORRALL THOMPSON

I am delighted to be involved in this project to raise funds for the Adopt a School Trust, a very worthwhile charity that focuses on the importance of getting children back into the kitchen and understanding food values.

I am also a great fan of frozen pastry as it is ideal to encourage people to experiment with baking by eliminating the dreaded 'fear factor' of failed pastry! It is a great way to ensure a perfect result every time and is there in the freezer for whenever inspiration – or necessity – strikes!

Makes 8

16 trimmed asparagus tips
1 x 425g Jus-Rol ready rolled puff pastry, thawed
    if frozen
1 egg yolk beaten with 1 teaspoon cold water
1 large red onion, finely sliced
1 clove of garlic, chopped
A small cube of butter
1 tablespoon olive oil
2 teaspoons balsamic vinegar
1 tablespoon golden caster sugar
250g assorted mushrooms, chopped
120g soft goat's cheese
Sea salt and freshly ground pepper

Preheat the oven to 200°C, Gas 6. Blanch the asparagus tips in a little boiling salted water for 2 minutes, then drain and run them under a gentle cold tap until cold. Drain and carefully pat dry with paper towel. Set aside.

Unroll and cut each pastry sheet into four for eight cases. Place on two non-stick baking sheets, brush the tops with the egg glaze then bake for about 18-20 minutes, checking they are browning evenly and turning the trays if necessary. (If you have only one sheet then bake these in two batches.)

Meanwhile, cook the onion and garlic in the butter and olive oil over a low heat for 15-20 minutes until caramelised and soft. Add the mushrooms, balsamic vinegar and sugar and cook for a couple more minutes, adding a little extra oil if necessary. Season to taste.

Spoon the onion and mushroom mixture into the pastry cases, crumble over the cheese and return them to the oven for about 5 minutes until the cheese melts a little. Place the asparagus tips on top and return for 2 more minutes to reheat, then serve.

Cheese Straws

ANNIE BELL

Children adore the creativity of cooking as much as painting, drawing and other crafts and pastry is the perfect material for young hands, with no need for saucepans, a safe way of letting their imagination run wild. A packet of ready-made pastry is a great rainy-day fallback.

Makes 20-25

Either - 1 x 212g sheet ready rolled puff pastry, thawed or 250g puff pastry, thawed
25g grated fresh Parmesan
25g grated Gruyère
a knife tip of cayenne pepper
1 egg yolk beaten with one tablespoon milk

Heat the oven to 190°C, Gas 5. Roll out the pastry as thinly as possible (about 1-2mm, the thickness of a 10p piece) on a lightly floured surface into a large rectangle about 30 x 50cm wide. Place the long sides facing you, and trim the edges to neaten.

Mix together the Parmesan and Gruyère with the cayenne pepper in a bowl and scatter over the top half of the pastry, leaving a 1cm edge.

Brush the edge with the egg wash and bring the lower half of pastry up over it to enclose the cheese. Press down on the edges to seal and lightly roll the pastry to compress the cheese, you should have a strip about 15cm wide. Cut this into 1cm wide straws.

Holding each strip with both hands, twist it to give 5 turns. Then lay 2cm apart on one or two non-stick baking sheets, pressing the ends well down so they don't unravel as they cook.

Bake for 12-15 minutes until an even gold colour, turning the trays round halfway through. The bottom tray may take a few minutes longer than the top.

Cool the trays for a few minutes then loosen the straws with a palette knife and slide onto a wire rack. (Any that break are *Cook's tips/treats*). They are best served freshly baked and still a little warm. I like to serve them stacked upright in a wide glass tumbler.

They can be stored for up to 4 days in an airtight container, and reheated for 5 minutes in a low oven.

Big Sausage and Apple Pastry

AMANDA GRANT

I am totally passionate about getting children into the kitchen. They need to be able to get messy with food, to touch, smell and learn about food and one of the best ways to do this is to let them get cooking. This big sausage pastry is really easy to make and tastes delicious. It is ideal for a weekday supper for the family or for when friends pop in. Try adding some cheese instead of the apple. Make sure you buy good quality sausage meat with a high percentage of pork - it will taste better and be better for you too.

Serves 4-6

1 tablespoon olive oil
450g prime quality sausage meat
1 large onion, finely chopped
1 clove garlic, crushed
2 dessert apples (e.g. Granny Smiths), cored and grated
2 sprigs fresh thyme
100ml apple juice
100ml vegetable stock
500g puff pastry, thawed if frozen
A little whole milk, to glaze
Freshly ground black pepper

Preheat the oven 200°C, Gas 6. Heat the oil in a heavy based pan and brown the sausage meat, stirring to break it up. Transfer to a plate.

Add the onion and garlic to the pan and gently fry until the onion is soft, about 5 minutes, then add the apples and fry for a few minutes more.

Return the meat to the pan with the thyme, apple juice, stock and some freshly ground black pepper then simmer until all the liquid is evaporated, about 10 minutes. Set aside to cool.

On a lightly floured surface, roll out the puff pastry into a large rectangle about 2.5mm thick then place pastry on a non-stick baking sheet. Brush round the outside edge with milk. Spoon the sausage mixture into the centre of the pastry, leaving a 2.5cm border all the way round. Bring the two short ends into the middle, overlapping slightly and pressing them well together. Pinch the long sides together. Brush the top with more milk and bake for 15-20 minutes, then lower the heat to 180°C, Gas 4 and cook for another 20 minutes until golden and risen. Cool for 15 minutes or so then serve cut in slices.

Pancetta, Egg and Feta Tarts

DAVID HERBERT

Serves 4

1 tablespoon olive oil, plus extra to brush
1 x 130g pack cubetti di pancetta or lardons
1 x 425g pack ready rolled puff pastry, thawed
    if frozen
50g feta cheese, crumbled
4 medium free-range eggs
Sea salt and freshly ground black pepper

Preheat the oven to 200°C, Gas 6. Lightly grease a non-stick baking tray.

Heat the oil in a frying pan over a medium heat, add the pancetta and cook, stirring occasionally, for 7 minutes or until it starts to colour. Drain on kitchen paper. Unroll the pastry and cut 4 x 13cm circles. Transfer the circles to the baking tray. Using the tip of a sharp knife, score a 2cm border around the inside of the pastry and cut three quarters of the way through (almost to the bottom of the pastry). Top each pastry circle with the pancetta and feta, keeping within the border. Brush the borders with a little more oil.

Bake for 7-10 minutes until the border has risen. Remove from the oven and gently push down the centres to make nests. Break an egg into the centre of each nest. Season lightly, as the feta and pancetta are already salty, and return to the oven. Cook for a further 5-7 minutes, or until the eggs are cooked to your liking and the pastry is golden. Cool for 10 minutes then serve hot with some salad.

Asparagus Filo Fingers

SUE McMAHON

These are ideal for children to help make.

Serves 4

1 tablespoon wholegrain mustard
2 tablespoons olive oil
4 slices Parma ham
12 thick asparagus spears, bases trimmed
2 sheets Jus-Rol filo pastry
To serve:
4 tomatoes
Extra virgin olive oil
Some fresh basil leaves
Sea salt and freshly ground black pepper

Preheat the oven to 200°C, Gas 6. Mix the mustard with a tablespoon of olive oil. Cut each slice of ham into 3 strips lengthways.

Using a swivel vegetable peeler peel off the tough ends of the asparagus if necessary. Then wrap a strip of Parma ham around each spear like a helter-skelter.

Cut each sheet of filo into strips the same size as the ham. Brush the mustard oil on one side of each filo strip then wrap each around the spears. Place the filo fingers on a non-stick baking sheet and brush with the remaining oil.

Bake towards the top of the oven for 15-20 minutes until the pastry is a light golden colour and crisp. Remove and cool for about 10 minutes then serve 3 per person.

Slice the tomatoes, season and arrange on four plates. Drizzle over more oil and scatter with the basil leaves. Arrange the filo fingers on each plate and serve. To serve as canapés, cut the fingers in half before baking.

The Ultimate Sausage Rolls

BRIAN TURNER CBE

As a true Yorkshireman, Brian has strong views on 'proper' sausage rolls. The meat must be the best quality sausage and the pastry melt in the mouth. Here, he gives it all a neat update by serving with a fresh tomato relish.

Makes about 6

250g puff pastry, thawed if frozen
1 garlic clove, crushed or finely chopped
1 tablespoon chopped fresh parsley
450-500g prime quality sausage meat
1 egg, beaten with a splash of water or milk
Sea salt and freshly ground black pepper, optional

Relish
$^{1}/_{2}$ teaspoon cumin seeds
About 250g tomatoes, chopped finely
1 bunch of spring onions
125g Greek yogurt
1 lime, $^{1}/_{2}$ grated zest and all the juice
$^{1}/_{2}$ small red chilli, seeded and chopped
4 tablespoons chopped fresh mint

Mix all the relish ingredients together in a bowl and leave in fridge for one hour.

Preheat the oven to 220°C, Gas 7 and lightly grease a baking sheet or line it with a sheet of baking parchment.

Roll out the pastry on a lightly floured board to a long strip 10cm wide and about the thickness of a £1 coin.

Mix the garlic and the parsley with the sausage meat and season lightly if liked. Roll into a sausage shape almost the same length as the pastry.

Lay this long sausage on top of the pastry just off centre, closer to one edge.

Brush the edges of the pastry with water, then fold the pastry over and seal well by pushing down carefully.

Brush the top with beaten egg wash, then score the top with a fork and brush again with egg wash. Cut the sausage roll into six smaller rolls.

Bake on the prepared sheet for about 25-30 minutes until golden brown and crisp, then slide onto a wire rack and cool for about 15 minutes. Serve the sausage rolls with the relish alongside.

Goat's Cheese, Leek and Tapenade Parcels

LULU GRIMES

These make a stunningly easy light meal, perfect for light summer lunches with a salad.

Serves 2

50g butter
2 leeks, trimmed and thinly sliced
4 sheets ready rolled filo pastry, 50 x 24cm
2 tablespoons tapenade
100g goat's cheese, either 1 Crottin or 2 thick
    slices from a log
2 small sprigs thyme

Preheat the oven to 180°C, Gas 4. Melt 30g of the butter in a saucepan, add the leeks and stir to coat them in the fat. Cook them gently over a low heat until they are completely tender. Leeks take much longer to cook than you might think – up to a good 10 minutes. Remove and cool.

Melt the rest of the butter in a bowl in the microwave, or in a small saucepan on the stove. Place one of the filo sheets on the work surface with the short end facing you. Brush with some butter. Lay another sheet right on top of it and cover it with cling film to stop the pastry drying out. Do the same with the other two sheets.

When the leeks are cool, uncover the filo. Spread the tapenade over the middle of each double layered pastry, leaving a wide border around the edges. Spoon the leeks on top of the tapenade, then place a goat's cheese roll and thyme sprig on top of that.

Now fold the bottom third of pastry up over the cheese and leeks and fold the two sides in, like an envelope. Fold the top third down to completely enclose the filling and roll the whole parcel over and place join side down on a non-stick baking sheet. Repeat with the other parcel. Brush both pastries with the rest of the butter and bake the parcels for 20 minutes. The pastry should be browned and crunchy and the filling melted and oozing. Cool a little before serving with a green salad.

Tomato Tarts

GORDON RAMSAY

Wonderful as a special make-ahead starter or light lunch.

Serves 4

1 x 425g pack ready rolled puff pastry, thawed
   if frozen
8 large ripe plum tomatoes, skinned
2 tablespoons olive oil
2 tablespoons balsamic vinegar
1 tablespoon chopped fresh parsley
1 tablespoon shredded fresh basil
50g fresh Parmesan, shaved with a swivel peeler
150g buffalo mozzarella
12-16 pitted black olives, sliced
100g wild rocket
1-2 tablespoons vinaigrette
Sea salt and freshly ground black pepper

Unroll the pastry sheets onto a board. Cut out four rounds about 12cm diameter, using a saucer or small plate as a guide. Place on a heavy baking sheet, prick the base several times and chill for 20 minutes. Meanwhile, preheat the oven to 200°C, Gas 6. Bake the pastry for 10 minutes then place a sheet of baking parchment and a heavy metal baking sheet on top to weigh it down and keep it flat. Bake for a further 10 minutes until just golden. Uncover and remove to a wire tray to crisp.

Slice the tomatoes evenly and arrange in four overlapping circles about the same size as the pastry rounds (certainly no larger) on another baking sheet. Brush with the oil and balsamic, season and sprinkle with the herbs. Lay shavings of Parmesan on top making sure they connect with all the slices. This is because as they melt the shavings hold the tomato together.

Preheat the grill to the highest setting and when really hot place the tomatoes under the grill near to the heat. The cheese should start to melt almost immediately. Watch carefully – the cheese doesn't need to burn just melt so it holds the tomato slices.

Remove from the grill, wait a few seconds then using a fish slice or palette knife scoop up each round of tomato on to a pastry round.

Slice the mozzarella or pull apart and pile on top. Season well and scatter over the olives. Season the rocket and toss with the dressing. Pile on top of each tart and serve immediately.

Chinatown Chicken Pies

JILL DUPLEIX

Advice to kids who like to cook: try to humour your parents and keep them calm as you cook. They are naturally nervous creatures and can be a nuisance, but well-handled, can be quite useful for things like doing the dishes.

Makes 12 to serve 4-6

6 fresh or dried shiitake mushrooms
Half a roasted or poached chicken, to give about
    250g cooked meat
2 tablespoons vegetable oil
4 shallots, or 1 small onion, finely sliced
1 tablespoon plain flour + extra for rolling
110ml chicken stock
1 tablespoon soy sauce
1 tablespoon oyster sauce
1 tablespoon hoi sin or plum sauce
2 tablespoons chopped fresh coriander leaves
500g pack puff pastry, thawed
1 egg yolk, beaten with 1 tablespoon milk

If using dried shiitake mushrooms, soak in hot water for 30 minutes then drain. Trim the stalks and slice the caps for either dried or fresh mushrooms.

Heat the oven to 200°C, Gas 6. Shred the meat from the chicken and chop it finely. Heat the oil in a wok or frying pan and cook the shallots or onion gently until softened, about 3-5 minutes.

Sprinkle in the flour and cook, stirring, for 1 minute and then gradually add the chicken stock, stirring. Add the mushrooms and the three sauces, then simmer for another 5 minutes. Remove from the heat, stir in the chicken and coriander and leave to cool. Cut the pastry in two and roll out each half, one at a time, on a lightly floured worktop to the thickness of a £1 coin (about 3mm). Cut into 24 x 12 cm squares and brush the edges with a little cold water. Place a tablespoon of the chicken mixture on to each of the squares. Top with the other squares and press down around the filling to seal. Press a large upturned glass or small Chinese bowl about 12cm diameter down firmly over the top to mark and trim the pies into neat circles. Place on a non-stick baking sheet or one lined with baking parchment and brush the tops with egg and milk glaze. Cut a small slash in the top and bake for 20 to 25 minutes or until golden, crisp and steaming hot.

Chutney, Pancetta and Thyme Tarts

LORNA WING

A jar of your favourite chutney thickly spread over crisp Jus-Rol puff pastry is a fantastic cheat's alternative to making your own base. I've used tomato, but it's brilliant, too, with a sticky onion chutney.

Makes 6

1 x 130g pack cubetti di pancetta
1 x 425g pack Jus-Rol ready rolled puff pastry, thawed if frozen
6 tablespoons tomato chutney
75g grated Parmesan
1 heaped tablespoon roughly chopped fresh thyme
Sea salt and freshly ground black pepper

Preheat the oven to 190°C, Gas 5. Fry the pancetta in a non-stick frying pan over a low heat for a couple of minutes until the fat starts to run, then increase the heat a little and cook for another 3 minutes until lightly coloured. Drain on paper towel and cool. Unroll the pastry, divide each sheet into 3 for 6 equal pieces and place on 2 non-stick baking trays. Spread the chutney almost to the edges, scatter over the cheese, pancetta and thyme. Season lightly and bake on the middle and top shelves for 12-15 minutes, swapping the trays over halfway through, until the pastry is risen and golden. Cool slightly before serving. Also good cold.

Chilli Garlic Lamb in Filo Pastry

PAUL RANKIN

These tasty samosa-like snacks are miles ahead of those found in some take-aways or supermarkets. More reminiscent of good Indian home cooking, they are easy to make yourself with good filo pastry as canapés or with a little salad and a light yogurt sauce for a first course.

Makes 12

1 tablespoon butter
1 small onion, finely chopped
200g lean minced lamb
3 cloves garlic, finely chopped
2 fresh green chillies, seeds removed, finely sliced
1 tablespoon chopped fresh ginger, chopped
$1/4$ teaspoon turmeric
A pinch of nutmeg
$1/4$ teaspoon garam masala or mild curry powder
1 tablespoon coriander leaves, chopped
1 teaspoon fresh lemon juice
3 sheets of filo pastry, 50 x 24cm
60g ghee or butter, melted
Sea salt and freshly ground black pepper

In a heavy frying pan melt the tablespoon of butter and fry the onion over moderate heat, until soft and light brown, about 5 minutes.

Add the mince, along with the garlic, chillies, ginger, turmeric, nutmeg and a little salt and stir fry for 3-4 minutes making sure the mince is nice and crumbly.

Add 2 tablespoons of water, cover and continue to cook gently for another 15 minutes, stirring occasionally. Uncover and cook for a few more minutes to reduce down any excess liquid. Remove from the heat, cool and add the garam masala, the chopped coriander leaves, salt and pepper and lemon juice.

Meanwhile, preheat the oven to 180°C, Gas 4. Work with one or two sheets of filo pastry at a time, keeping the rest covered with a damp cloth or cling film to keep them from drying out.

Cut each filo sheet into half lengthways, and then fold each piece in half lengthways again for 6 long doubled strips. Now cut these strips in half for 12 strips. Brush the pastry lightly with ghee or butter. Put a full teaspoon of the mince mixture in one corner at the bottom of a strip of pastry. Fold the pastry from the other corner over it so you have a short diagonal fold, then flip the enclosed filling upward and over again at right angles several times until you reach the top and have a neat wrapped triangle.

Lightly brush all over with ghee and put on a greased baking sheet. Repeat the process until you have 12 parcels. Bake them for 10 minutes, then brush again with the remaining ghee and return to the oven for a further 5 minutes. Allow to cool for 10 minutes before serving.

Goat's Cheese with Sesame Seeds in Filo

PRUE LEITH OBE

Serves 6

6 small (50g) or 3 medium (100g) goat's cheeses
   (e.g Crottins)
85g sesame seeds, lightly toasted
3 large sheets filo pastry
30g butter, melted
2 heads radicchio, chicory or rocket

Dressing
2 tablespoons olive oil
2 tablespoons white wine vinegar
1 clove garlic, crushed
2 tablespoons chopped fresh chives
salt and freshly ground black pepper

Preheat the oven to 200°C, Gas 6. If you are using medium size goat's cheeses, cut them in half horizontally. Roll the cheese in the sesame seeds until completely coated. Spread out the filo pastry, brush with melted butter and cut into 12 x 15cm squares. Layer one square on top of another for 6 double layers. Place a goat's cheese in the centre of each square and brush the edges lightly with some water. Draw up the pastry to form a bag and press hard to seal the edges together. Lightly dot the outside of the pastry with melted butter, place on a non-stick baking sheet and bake in the preheated oven for 5-7 minutes until golden brown. Meanwhile, beat all ingredients for the dressing together. Separate the radicchio, chicory or rocket into leaves and toss in the dressing. Arrange the leaves on six serving plates and place the filo parcels on top. Serve immediately.

Crab and Gruyère Tartlets

RICK STEIN

Serves 4

350g shortcrust pastry, thawed if frozen
    (³/₄ x 500g pack)
1 egg white
225g fresh white crab meat
50g fresh brown crab meat
2 egg yolks
85ml double cream
A pinch of cayenne pepper
50g Gruyere cheese, finely grated
Sea salt and freshly ground black pepper

Preheat the oven to 220°C, Gas 7. Briefly knead the pastry on a lightly floured surface until smooth and cut into four equal pieces. Roll each of these to rounds approximately 17-18cm diameter. Gently lift into 4 x 11cm loose base tartlet tins, about 2cm deep. Press well into the sides and trim the tops neatly with a sharp knife. Chill for 20 minutes.

Line each pastry case with crumpled baking parchment paper, cover the base with a generous layer of baking beans. Place on a heavy metal tray and bake blind (see page 9) for 15 minutes. Remove the paper and beans, brush the inside of each pastry case with a little unbeaten egg white and return to the oven for 2 minutes. Remove from the oven and lower the temperature to 200°C, Gas 6.

Mix the crab meat with egg yolks, cream, cayenne and some salt and pepper. Spoon the mixture into the tartlet cases and sprinkle with the grated gruyère cheese. Bake at the top of the oven for 15-20 minutes until lightly golden. Serve warm as a starter or cold for picnics.

Prawn Cocktail Vol-au-Vent

ROZ DENNY

These pastry cases, which are best cooked from frozen, can be baked and cooled ahead, then the filling made just before serving. A 1960s favourite that has become a classic of the buffet tray.

Makes 18

¹/₂ pack Jus-Rol Vol-au-Vent (18 pastry cases)
1 egg yolk + ¹/₂ teaspoon cold water
250g king size peeled prawns, thawed if frozen
1 clove garlic, crushed
2 tablespoons olive oil
2 pinches ground cumin
Juice of 1 lime
1 small ripe avocado
2 tablespoons mayonnaise
2 tablespoons crème fraîche (not half fat)
1 tablespoon tomato purée
2 dashes Worcestershire sauce or mild chilli relish
1 tablespoon chopped fresh coriander or parsley
Freshly ground black pepper
To garnish, small coriander or parsley leaves or
    quarters of cherry tomato (optional)

Heat the oven to 220°C, Gas 7. Lay the vol-au-vent on a non-stick baking tray or one lined with baking parchment. Brush the edges with the egg yolk. Bake for about 15 minutes, turning once until evenly golden.

Remove, cool a little and using a small sharp knife, ease off the tops and scoop out any uncooked pastry. Return the cases to the oven to dry out for 2 minutes, then cool.

Stir fry the prawns with the garlic in the oil for about 5 minutes until cooked and pink. Mix in the cumin and squeeze over the lime juice. Remove and cool.

Peel and halve the avocado. Cut a quarter into 18 neat slices for garnish. Chop the rest.

When the prawns have cooled, cut the tails off 18 to use as garnish. Chop the rest.

Mix together the mayo, crème fraîche, tomato purée, sauce or relish and chopped herbs. Season with pepper only. Mix in the chopped prawns and avocado.

When ready to serve, spoon into the pastry shells using a teaspoon. Top each shell with a prawn tail and avocado slice. Garnish with herb leaves and tomato pieces, if using.

Aubergine, Pepper and Spiced Feta Tart

YVONNE ALLISON

Serves 6

1 medium aubergine, cut in 3mm slices
1 orange or yellow pepper, cored, seeded and
    cut in strips
A little olive oil, to brush
1 x 500g pack Jus-Rol puff pastry, thawed
2 eggs
2 egg yolks
200ml Greek yogurt
200g feta, crumbled
2 cloves garlic, peeled and crushed
1$\frac{1}{2}$ teaspoons fennel seeds
1 teaspoon coriander seeds, crushed
A pinch of paprika
Sea salt and freshly ground black pepper

Heat oven to 190°C, Gas 5. Lightly brush both sides of the aubergine slices and the pepper strips with olive oil and lay them on a large baking sheet. Roast for about 20 minutes until tender.

Roll out the pastry to 3mm thickness (like a £1 coin). Lift into a 22cm tart tin and press well into the sides, trimming the edges allowing a little overhang. Prick the base, place the tin on a metal baking sheet and bake for 10 minutes. Remove and prick the base again and using a large spoon press the puffed layers down gently until flat. Bake for 10 more minutes and press down again on the base.

Whisk together the eggs, egg yolks and yogurt. Mix the feta with the garlic, fennel and coriander seeds and combine with the egg and yogurt mix. Season, adding salt cautiously because of the feta.

When the pastry case is golden brown and crisp, cover the base with overlapping slices of aubergine and half the strips of the pepper. Reserve one small slice of aubergine.

Pour over the feta, egg and yogurt mix. Arrange the rest of the pepper strips in 'spokes' on the top and place the aubergine slice in the centre. Sprinkle over the paprika and return to the oven to bake for about 25 minutes until risen and golden. Cool before slicing.

Lamb and Rosemary Envelopes

MARY CADOGAN

I have always enjoyed cooking with children and I find pastry is a particular pleasure as it is fun to roll out and handle and they can cut their own shapes for decoration. I also found that when my own sons were young they were always more likely to eat something they had a hand in preparing, than food that was plonked in front of them.

Serves 4

4 boneless lamb leg steaks, about 100g each
Leaves from 3 sprigs of rosemary, chopped, plus 4 small sprigs for garnish
1 tablespoon olive or sunflower oil
1 x 425g pack ready rolled puff pastry, thawed if frozen
4 rounded tablespoons cranberry sauce
1 egg, beaten
Sea salt and freshly ground pepper

Season the lamb steaks on both sides with salt and freshly ground pepper and sprinkle with the chopped rosemary. Heat the oil in a large, heavy-based frying pan and brown the lamb steaks for 2 minutes on each side. Transfer to a plate and leave to cool.

Cut each puff pastry sheet into two so you have four even-sized rectangles, approximately 14 x 21cm. Place a cooled lamb steak on each piece of pastry, then top each with a tablespoon of cranberry sauce.

Brush the pastry edges with some of the egg, then fold over to enclose the lamb, pinching the edges to seal. Place the lamb parcels on a lightly greased non-stick baking sheet and chill for 20 minutes whilst you preheat the oven to 200°C, Gas 6.

Brush the parcels with beaten egg, top each one with a rosemary sprig and bake for 20-25 minutes until puffed and golden. Allow to stand for 10 minutes at least before serving.

Moroccan Spiced Pie

ANGELA NILSEN

Pastry making has always been a bit of a passion with me. In fact it was the first thing I ever made, aged about eight, when an aunt gave me a pastry set for my birthday. Since then, the convenience of ready-made pastry has made it an even easier way to introduce the pleasures of cooking to children.

Serves 6-8

1 teaspoon each coriander and cumin seeds
1 teaspoon paprika, plus extra for dusting
$\frac{1}{2}$ teaspoon ground cinnamon
150ml olive oil
1 squash (about 900g-1kg), peeled, seeded and
    cut into 2cm chunks
12 shallots, peeled and quartered
4cm piece root ginger, finely chopped
140g whole blanched almonds
140g shelled pistachios
75g pack dried cranberries
6 tablespoons clear honey
1 x 225g-250g pack fresh leaf spinach
1 x 400g can chickpeas, drained and rinsed
2 garlic cloves
1 teaspoon ground cumin
3 tablespoons lemon juice
4 tablespoons chopped fresh coriander
100g butter
8 large sheets filo pastry, 50 x 24cm, thawed
    if frozen
1 lemon, cut into 8 wedges, to serve

Harissa Yogurt Sauce
200g carton Greek yogurt
6 tablespoons milk
A good handful fresh coriander, chopped
2-3 teaspoons harissa paste

Preheat the oven to 200°C, Gas 6. Dry fry the seeds briefly in a small pan over a medium heat until toasty – don't let them burn. Then grind coarsely using a pestle and mortar (or use a bowl and the end of a rolling pin), or pulse in a spice mill or small food processor. Mix with the paprika, cinnamon, $\frac{1}{2}$ tsp salt and 4 tablespoons of the oil. Toss in the squash chunks and tip into a roasting tin adding seasoning to taste. Roast for about 20 minutes until just tender, stirring once or twice. Remove from the oven (if you are making this pie ahead the oven can be turned off at this point).

Meanwhile, heat another 2 tablespoons of oil in a frying pan, add the shallots and cook, stirring until they start to brown. Stir in the ginger and 100g each of the almonds and pistachios. When lightly browned, toss in the cranberries, 2 tablespoons honey and the spinach, stirring until it wilts. Take off the heat and stir into the roasted squash then set aside to cool.

Make a houmous by whizzing together in a food processor the chickpeas, garlic, ground cumin, remaining oil, lemon juice, 2 tablespoons water, salt and pepper. Mix in the chopped coriander by hand.

When ready to put the pie together reheat the oven to 200°C, Gas 6 if it isn't already on. Melt the

butter in a small pan. Place a loose-bottomed 28cm quiche tin on a baking sheet and brush with some butter. Keeping the filo covered with a damp cloth or cling film so it doesn't dry out, lay one sheet over half of the tin so that it hangs over the edge by about 10cm. Lay another sheet on the other side, so it overlaps the first in the centre and hangs over the opposite edge. Brush with butter. Lay two more filo sheets in the opposite direction in the same way and brush with more butter. Build up two more layers in this way, so you use a total of eight sheets of filo.

Pile half the squash mixture in the centre of the pastry. Spread over the houmous and then the rest of the squash mixture. One at a time, bring the edge of each filo sheet up to the centre to cover the filling, creating voluptuous folds as you go. Brush carefully with more butter. (*If making a day ahead, cover now with cling film and chill. To reheat, remove the pie from the fridge, heat the oven, then bake for 35-40 minutes.*)

Bake for 30-35 minutes, until crisp and golden. Just before the pie is ready, reheat any remaining butter in the pan, tip in the rest of the nuts and fry until golden.

Spoon in the 4 remaining tablespoons of honey and, when it melts, take off the heat and pour over the pie. Serve with the harissa yogurt sauce and lemon wedges.

To make the sauce, mix the yogurt and milk together to make a thin sauce, stir in the coriander and season. Swirl in the harissa to taste.

No-Roll Chicken and Mushroom Pastries

BARNEY DESMAZERY

My Christmas holidays often include a few days in Paris. As the French don't really 'do' breakfast like we do, I find myself famished around mid-morning. What a pleasure to walk into a boulangerie and see all those savoury squares of puff pastry with different fillings and toppings like leek and goat's cheese, the sort of flavour combinations that wouldn't be out of place on the menu in the local bistro. Back home this is the sort of thing I make for myself on Friday night and snack on throughout the weekend. Don't be put off by the pastry element of this, I've used those clever packs of ready-rolled pastry so you don't have to do any rolling.

Makes 4

4 tablespoons olive oil
250g pack chestnut mushrooms, sliced
About 2 tablespoons chopped fresh parsley
1 plump clove garlic, crushed
1 x 425g pack ready-rolled puff pastry, thawed
   if frozen
4 skinless, boneless chicken breasts, about
   140g each
1 free range egg, beaten
Sea salt and freshly ground black pepper

Preheat the oven to 220°C, Gas 7. Place a heavy metal baking tray in the oven at the same time.

Heat half the oil in a frying pan, then throw in the mushrooms and fry over a high heat for about 3 minutes until lightly browned. Season generously and toss in the parsley and garlic.

Unroll the pastry sheets and cut each in half. Sit a chicken breast in the middle of each pastry piece on the long diagonal. Spoon over the mushrooms and drizzle with the remaining oil.

Bring the two longer corners together in the middle and dab with some egg. Press together to seal. Brush the remaining pastry with more egg.

Remove the hot baking tray and place the chicken pastries on top. Return and bake for 20 minutes or until the chicken is just cooked. Allow to cool for about 5 minutes then serve.

Mushroom, Leek and Chestnut Jalousie

SHONA CRAWFORD POOLE

Serves 4

500g small or medium size leeks
75g butter, melted
250g button mushrooms
1 tablespoon fresh lemon juice
200g cooked and peeled chestnuts, halved if large
1 large onion, finely chopped
50g wild or open cap mushrooms, finely chopped
100g fresh white breadcrumbs
2 tablespoons finely chopped parsley
$\frac{1}{2}$ teaspoon fresh thyme leaves or a good pinch of chopped fresh tarragon
500g pack puff pastry, thawed if frozen
1 egg yolk beaten with 1 tablespoon milk
Sea salt and freshly ground pepper

Top and tail the leeks and cut them into 2cm thick chunks. Steam until almost tender, about 5 minutes, then transfer to a large bowl and leave to cool.

Pour a third of the melted butter into a wide pan and add the button mushrooms. Sauté over a high heat, stirring until they are beginning to brown, then season with salt, pepper and lemon juice. Mix the mushrooms with the leeks and return the pan to cook off any liquid until reduced and syrupy. Set aside until completely cold.

Add the chestnuts and another third of melted butter, season generously and mix carefully so that the leeks and chestnuts do not break up. Set aside until cold.

Gently fry the onion in another pan with the last of the butter and cook slowly until the onion is tender, but not coloured. Raise the heat and add the finely chopped wild or open cap mushrooms. Fry for two or three minutes, stirring until the mushrooms are cooked. Take the pan off the heat and stir in the breadcrumbs and chopped herbs. Season the mixture well, then set aside until completely cold.

Roll out the pastry to a rectangle about 50cm x 25cm and divide into two so you now have 2 x 25cm squares. Lay one square of pastry on a baking sheet lined with baking parchment and divide the finely chopped bread and wild mushroom mixture on top. Spoon over the leek and mushroom mixture and brush the edges with a little cold water.

Cut slashes in the remaining square of pastry and lay over the first square, taking care not to stretch the dough. Press the edges of the pastry together to seal, trim and crimp.

Chill for about 30 minutes whilst you heat the oven to 220°C, Gas 7. Just before baking, brush the jalousie with the egg and milk glaze and bake for about 30 minutes, until crisp and golden.

Bruno's Pie

DEBORA ROBERTSON

I see having some Jus-Rol in my freezer as a sort of culinary insurance policy for those times when people pop round for drinks and it suddenly turns into dinner, or against those gloomy days when you get home from work and only something delicious encased in pastry is going to hit the spot! It also has a soothing familiarity about it - I'm sure one of the first things I ever cooked as a very young girl was jam tarts made with Jus-Rol pastry, standing on a stool to reach the counter. As I was thinking about a recipe to contribute to *A Passion for Pastry*, my husband reminded me of our best 'Jus-Rol to the rescue' moment.

I came up with this recipe a couple of years ago when, on Christmas morning while happily expecting our 18 guests, I suddenly remembered that my husband's cousin was a vegetarian and probably wouldn't want to tuck into the goose. So I scrambled around in the fridge and freezer and found the ingredients and hastily threw them together. Bruno's Pie was born – loosely based around my favourite sandwich filling at our local Italian deli! We like to serve it warm for lunch or eat it cold for a picnic.

Serves 4-6

500g fresh spinach, (or frozen and thawed)
3 hard-boiled eggs, roughly chopped
275g mozzarella, cut into 5mm dice
30g freshly grated Parmesan
30g toasted pine nuts
2 tablespoons single cream
1 large egg, lightly beaten
1 teaspoon freshly ground black pepper
$1/2$ teaspoon sea salt
$1/2$ teaspoon freshly grated nutmeg
500g shortcrust pastry, thawed if frozen
A little milk, for brushing

Preheat the oven to 200°C, Gas 6. Lightly grease a non-stick baking sheet or line it with a sheet of baking parchment.

Blanch the fresh spinach, if using, in boiling water for 1-2 minutes then drain and cool. Wrap the cooked or frozen spinach in several layers of kitchen paper or clean tea towel and squeeze dry, then chop roughly.

In a mixing bowl, combine the spinach, chopped eggs, mozzarella, Parmesan, pine nuts, single cream, three quarters of the beaten egg (reserve the rest for glazing) plus pepper, salt and nutmeg. Stir until thoroughly combined.

Cut the pastry in two, with one piece fractionally larger than the other. Roll out the smaller piece on a lightly floured board until it measures 20 x 30cm and

place it on the prepared baking sheet. Roll out the second piece so that it measures approximately 22 x 32cm.

Place the spinach filling along the middle of the smaller piece of pastry and press it gently with your hands, leaving approximately 4cm of pastry clear around the sides of the filling. Brush the edges with a little milk.

Place the larger sheet of pastry over the top of the mixture, pressing the edges of the pastry gently together. Trim the edges and crimp to seal. Make 3 diagonal cuts, about 4-5cm long, along the top of the pie. Leave to rest in the fridge for 15-30 minutes. You can make the pie about 4 hours ahead to this point if you wish.

Brush the pie top with the remaining beaten egg and bake for 30-35 minutes, until golden. Slide onto a wire rack to cool for 15 minutes then serve warm or cold.

Smoked Trout Tart

MOYRA FRASER

Serves 6

1 x 28cm ready rolled shortcrust pastry sheet,
   thawed
A medium pinch of saffron threads
2 medium eggs, plus 1 medium egg yolk
200ml tub full-fat crème fraîche
2 level tablespoons freshly chopped chives
200g smoked trout, skinned roughly torn into
   strips
Sea salt and freshly ground pepper

Unroll the pastry and using a rolling pin, lift the dough into a 23cm flan tin or dish and press well into the sides. Follow instructions for baking blind on page 9. For the filling, turn the oven to 180°C, Gas 4. Put the saffron in a cup and stir in two teaspoons of boiling water. Infuse for 5 minutes.

Beat together the eggs, egg yolk, crème fraîche, saffron liquid and chives and season well with black pepper and lightly with salt. Pour the egg mixture into the tart case, then dot the trout on top. Carefully return the tart case to the oven on a baking sheet and cook for 30 minutes or until the filling is set but still slightly wobbly. Cool for 15 minutes and serve warm.

Caramelised Red Onion, Chicory and Devon Blue Cheese Tart

FIONA BECKETT

A really simple tart that makes a great centrepiece for a vegetarian meal or a dinner party starter for six. I make this with a soft blue cheese like Devon Blue or the famous Irish Cashel Blue but you could use Stilton.

Serves 4 as a main course or 6 as a starter

2 tablespoons olive oil

4 red onions (about 100g each), peeled and finely sliced

40g butter

1 teaspoon balsamic vinegar

6 medium sized heads of chicory (2 x 200g packs)

Juice of half a lemon

1 tablespoon golden caster sugar

350g puff pastry, thawed if frozen ($^3/_4$ x 500g pack)

1 egg yolk

175g soft blue cheese

Heat a large deep frying pan, add the oil and fry the onions over a moderate to high heat for about 10 minutes or until softened and lightly caramelised. Add a third of the butter and continue to fry, stirring, until well caramelised (about another 5 minutes). Season with the balsamic vinegar, salt and pepper.

Preheat the oven to 220°C, Gas 7. Tip the onions onto a plate to cool, wipe out the pan and return it to the heat. Trim the bottom off each head of chicory and cut it in half lengthways. Put the lemon juice and 4 tablespoons of water in the frying pan along with the remaining butter and the sugar. Heat gently until the sugar has dissolved.

Place the chicory pieces cut side up in the pan, turning them to coat in the lemon and butter mixture. This also stops them from discolouring. Bring to the boil, then cover the pan and cook for 5 minutes then turn them over and cook for another 5 minutes. Take the lid off the pan, turn the heat up slightly and bubble until the liquid reduces to a caramelised glaze, about another 5 minutes.

Roll out the pastry to a large rectangle, about 5mm thick, that will fit comfortably on a greased or non-stick baking sheet. Trim the edges to neaten. With a sharp knife score a line around the edge of the pastry about 1.5cm from the edge to create a rim, but take care not to cut through the pastry. Beat the egg yolk with a teaspoon of cold water and brush over the edge and the base of the tart taking care not to brush over the score line.

Spread the caramelised onions over the base then place the chicory down the middle alternating from side to side so that the tips meet in the centre. Pour over any remaining pan juices, season with a little salt and pepper and crumble the cheese over the top.

Bake for 10 minutes then reduce the heat to 180°C, Gas 4 and bake for a further 15-20 minutes until the tart is well puffed up around the edges and the top is nicely browned and crisp. Serve with a watercress or spinach salad.

Game Pies

MICHEL ROUX JUNIOR

Although I have specified a mixture of game you could use just one type, except for grouse which tends to be a little strong, so use slightly less and increase the pork shoulder accordingly. As the meat is minced, second quality, damaged or old game can be used.

Makes 12 small ones

1kg trimmed game meat (wild rabbit, venison, hare, grouse, pheasant)
400g pork belly
800g pork back fat
250g lean pork shoulder
A little brandy, to taste
1.5kg puff pastry
12 medallions (3cm x 2cm) of venison loin
150g cooked foie gras (optional), cut into 12 pieces
1 egg, beaten
Salt, pepper and nutmeg

Check the meat is free of bones and big pieces of sinew. Using a sharp knife remove the rind from the pork belly and the back fat. Cut the game and all the pork into 2cm dice, season well with salt, pepper, a little nutmeg and a generous splash of brandy, mix thoroughly, cover with cling film and chill for at least 36 hours – but for no more than 72 hours.

Put the marinated meats through a medium-sized hole on the mincer to make the forcemeat.

Take a third of this mixture and push it through the mincer again, keeping everything as cold as possible, then mix by hand with the rest of the forcemeat. Fry a little patty of forcemeat for a few minutes to check for seasoning.

Roll out the pastry to 2mm thick and cut out 12 x 15cm discs. Divide the forcemeat into 24 balls and place one on each disc. Push a piece of venison – and foie gras if you are using it – into half the balls and top with more forcemeat; this should come to about 3cm from the edge of the pastry.

Brush the edge of the pastry with beaten egg, then fold over to completely seal and envelop the forcemeat like a flat pasty. Pinch the pastry well to seal, then place, seal side down, on a baking sheet lined with non-stick baking parchment. Chill to rest for at least one hour.

Meanwhile, heat the oven to 180°C, Gas 4. Brush the pastry with more beaten egg. Cook for 25 minutes or until hot in the middle; test by inserting a darning needle for six seconds. It should feel piping hot.

Serve the pies hot or cold with salad. Perfect for a smart picnic.

The Almost 10 Minute Tart

MITZIE WILSON

This is one of my favourite quick recipes. It's as easy as pie to make – just unroll some puff pastry and top with your favourite fillings – tomato and goat's cheese, salami, olives and tomatoes, pesto and mozzarella. You could even make sweet versions such as apple slices and raisins with a dust of cinnamon, apricots and grated marzipan – whatever combination you fancy – and remember to vary the shape too, rounds, squares, mini or maxi size, depending on the occasion.

Serves 4

425g pack ready rolled puff pastry, thawed if
    frozen
Plain flour, for dusting
150g goat's cheese
250g vine cherry tomatoes, halved
1 egg, beaten with a little water
Extra-virgin olive oil, for drizzling
Large sprigs basil leaves, to garnish
4 slices Parma ham (optional)
Rocket, to serve

Preheat the oven to 200ºC, Gas 6. Open out the pastry on a surface lightly dusted with flour. Cut the pastry to make 4, equal-size squares/rectangles and put on two non-stick baking trays or ones lined with a sheet of baking parchment. Chill until ready to bake.

Break the cheese into craggy pieces. Arrange the tomato halves and goat's cheese in the centre of each pastry square. Don't worry if the piles look quite high, the pastry will cook up around them. Season well, then brush the edges with the beaten egg and pop in the oven for 15-18 minutes until puffed and golden.

Serve as they are, hot from the oven, drizzled with a little olive oil and garnished with a large basil sprig. Or top each tart with a slice of Parma ham before garnishing with either basil or rocket. Nice drizzled with a little runny pesto.

Potato, Onion and Soft Cheese Pie

NICHOLA PALMER

A delicious and homely style vegetarian main course which can be made ahead and baked freshly to serve hot, or chilled for picnics and lunch boxes.

Serves 4-6

500g puff pastry, thawed
550g potatoes, peeled and thinly sliced
1 medium onion, peeled and thinly sliced
1 x 200g tub full-fat soft cheese, plain or garlic
    and herb flavoured
1 x 15g packet fresh chives, chopped
Milk to glaze
Mixed salad, to serve
Sea salt and freshly ground pepper

Preheat the oven to 200°C, Gas 6. Roll out two-thirds of the pastry on a lightly floured surface to a 3mm thickness (like a £1 coin). Lifting up with a rolling pin, use to line a 20 round x 3cm deep loose-based tart tin.

Crumble up the cheese roughly and layer with the potatoes and onion into the pastry case, sprinkling salt, pepper and chopped chives between each layer. Finish with a layer of potatoes. Roll out the remaining pastry; brush the edge with water and lift over the filling to cover. Press the edges well together to seal and crimp, then trim off any excess pastry. Brush with milk and make a steam hole in the top.

Place on a heavy baking sheet and bake for 25 minutes until golden. Then reduce the oven temperature to 170°C, Gas 3 and cook for a further hour. Leave to stand for at least 20 minutes before turning out onto a flat plate or board and cutting into wedges. Perfect with a nicely dressed mixed salad.

Turkey, Leek and Gammon En Croute

WENDY SWEETSER

An impressive pie, ideal for a Boxing Day centrepiece or a smart picnic.

Serves 8

2 tablespoons sunflower oil
1 leek, trimmed and thinly sliced
250g gammon steak, snipped into small pieces
50g fresh breadcrumbs
225g herby sausage meat
1 teaspoon Dijon mustard
2 tablespoons sun-dried tomato purée
2 free range eggs, beaten, plus 1 extra, to glaze
350g turkey breast steaks
500g shortcrust pastry, thawed if frozen
Freshly ground black pepper

Preheat the oven to 170°C, Gas 3. Grease a 1kg loaf tin and line base and sides with baking parchment.

Heat the oil in a pan and fry the leek over a gentle heat until soft, about 5 minutes. Tip it into a bowl and mix in the gammon, breadcrumbs, sausage meat, mustard and sun-dried tomato puree. Stir in 2 eggs until the ingredients are evenly mixed and season with freshly ground black pepper only. (There is salt in the gammon.)

Spoon one third of the mixture into the loaf tin and spread level. Place half the turkey steaks on top and spoon over another third of the gammon mixture. Top with the remaining turkey and the rest of the gammon mixture. Cover with baking parchment and foil, tucking the edges of the foil around the lip of the tin to make a tight seal. Stand the tin in a roasting tray and pour in enough warm water to come half way up the sides. Cook in the oven for 1½ hours. Remove the tin from the oven. Cut a piece of heavy card that fits inside the tin and weigh it down with weights or 2 cans. This helps firm the filling. Leave until quite cold, at least 4 hours, then turn the loaf out of the tin.

Roll out about one-third of the pastry on a lightly floured work surface to an oblong about 3cm larger than the base of the loaf. Lift this onto a baking sheet lined with baking parchment. Place the loaf in the centre and trim the pastry to leave a 2cm border around the loaf. Beat the extra egg and use to brush the borders.

Roll out the remaining pastry and lift it over the loaf, using the rolling pin and allow to gently fall on top, pressing into the sides for a snug fit then pressing down on the edges to seal. Trim away excess pastry leaving a neat 1.5cm border. If liked, you can cut leaves or other decorations from the pastry trimmings and press them in place with dabs of glaze. Make 2 or 3 holes in the top of the pastry to allow steam to escape and chill the loaf for 30 minutes.

Meanwhile, preheat the oven to 200°C, Gas 6. Brush the loaf evenly with beaten egg and bake for 25-30 minutes until golden brown. Allow to stand for a good 10 minutes before slicing to serve. Good also served cold, but do not reheat leftovers.

Smoked Haddock and Watercress Tart

SUE LAWRENCE

Encouraging children to cook is crucial, not only to help them understand about quality ingredients and what fun it is to cook (albeit a little messy!) but most importantly, that there is absolutely nothing to better the taste of home cooking.

Serves 4-6

350g shortcrust pastry (³/₄ x 500g pack), thawed
   if frozen
about 400g undyed smoked haddock fillets
200ml milk
150ml double cream
2 large free range eggs
3-4 tablespoons watercress, chopped
1 heaped tablespoon freshly grated Parmesan
A few sunblushed tomatoes, optional, to serve
Sea salt and freshly ground black pepper

Heat the oven to 190°C, Gas 5. Roll out the pastry on a lightly floured surface to a 4mm thickness and line a shallow 28cm tart tin with a removable base. Press the pastry into the edges and trim the top allowing the pastry to extend slightly above the rim. Prick the base and chill again. Line the tart tin with baking parchment or foil and baking beans and place on a metal baking sheet. Then bake blind (see page 9) for 15 minutes. Remove the paper or foil and beans and continue to bake for a further 5 minutes. Remove and cool.

Meanwhile, poach the haddock in the milk for 3-4 minutes then drain in a sieve, reserving the liquid in a bowl. Allow to cool for 5 minutes then beat in the cream, eggs, watercress, Parmesan and salt and pepper to taste (I know it does not seem pleasant tasting raw custard but it is essential, because some curing of smoked haddock is saltier than others).

Flake the fish into the tart case and slowly pour over the filling. Bake for 30-40 minutes or until set and tinged with golden brown. For extra colour add some snipped sunblushed tomatoes on top halfway through the baking time. Eat warm with salad.

Artichoke Pie

JAMIE OLIVER

**Serves 6 as a main course or
12 in fingers for a buffet**

10 young globe artichokes *
4 egg yolks
A handful of grated pecorino cheese (about 30g)
A handful of grated Parmesan cheese (about 30g)
Zest of 1 lemon
A few sprigs of mint, torn
6-8 tablespoons olive oil
270g pack filo pastry, thawed if frozen
Sea salt and freshly ground black pepper

Trim the artichoke stems to about 2cm. Cook artichokes whole in plenty of boiling, salted water for about 30 minutes until the bases are tender when you push in a sharp knife. Drain them upside down and cool, then strip the leaves back until you get to pale purple-tipped delicate ones that are tender enough to eat. Slice off the top 1cm pointy tips of the leaves. Then cut the heart in half lengthways, and using a teaspoon scoop out and discard the hairy choke inside.

Using a fork roughly mash half the artichoke hearts in a bowl to a chunky purée and beat with the egg yolks, cheeses, lemon zest and seasoning (easy on the salt because of the cheese). Slice the remaining artichokes into 1cm strips and stir them into the mixture together with the torn mint leaves.

Preheat the oven to 180°C, Gas 4 whilst you make the pie. Pour the oil into a cup. Place a sheet of filo pastry on a worktop and brush lightly with oil. You have to work quite quickly with filo or it dries up and cracks, so don't hang about! Cover it with another sheet at a slightly different angle and repeat until the filo is 6 sheets thick.

Carefully lift up the oiled filo and place it in a 20cm baking tin or dish, gently pushing the pastry into the bottom. Spoon in the artichoke filling, then fold the sheets individually over the top of each other, scrunching attractively.

Brush the top with more oil and place the dish on a metal baking sheet. Bake the pie in the oven for 30 minutes until golden brown. Cool for 10 minutes before sliding out of the tin or dish to cut up and serve.

* If using larger artichokes, buy 6 around 350g each. Trim the stems close to the base, boil for 45 minutes then pull off all the leaves and scrape off the hairy choke to reveal the tender heart inside.

Crab and Rice Noodle Quiche

MICHEL ROUX SENIOR

This unusual quiche is creamy without being too rich. It is best served warm, rather than piping hot, to appreciate the delicate flavour of the crab, with a side salad of peppery rocket leaves.

Serves 8-10

1 crab, about 2kg, preferably live, or 300g fresh
    white crab meat
300g shortcrust pastry ($^2/_3$ x 500g pack)
flour for dusting
1 egg yolk mixed with 1 tablespoon milk (egg
    wash)
30g rice noodles
1 teaspoon English mustard powder
250ml milk
175ml double cream
3 eggs, plus 2 yolks
Salt and cayenne pepper
12 coriander leaves

If using a live crab, scrub lightly to remove any silt from the shell, then plunge into a pan of lightly salted water and cook for 10 minutes. Turn off the heat and leave the crab in the water for 20 minutes, then take it out and leave to cool for at least 1 hour. When the crab is cold, break off the legs and claws, lift off the top carapace, scrape out and reserve all the white meat, taking care to pick out any bits of shell and cartilage. You should have about 300g white meat. Scrape out the firmish brown meat from the carapace and keep it in a bowl.

Roll out the pastry on a lightly floured surface to a thickness of 3mm and use to line a greased 20cm flan ring, 4cm deep, placed on a baking sheet. Chill the pastry case in the fridge for 20 minutes. Preheat the oven to 200°C, Gas 6. Prick the chilled pastry case in several places with a fork. Line it with grease proof paper or foil, then fill with dried or ceramic baking beans. Bake for 20 minutes, then remove the beans and paper or foil. Lightly brush the pastry base with egg-wash and return to the oven for 3 minutes.

Put the rice noodles in a bowl and pour on lightly salted boiling water to cover. Leave for 15 minutes, then drain, refresh and pat dry with a tea towel. Cut the noodles into 5cm lengths and mix delicately with the white crab meat. Whisk together the mustard and milk then blend in the cream, eggs and egg yolks, and season with salt and cayenne pepper.

When ready to bake, set the oven to 170°C, Gas 3. Half-fill the pastry case with the crab meat and noodle mixture, and scatter small pieces of dark crab meat on top. Fill with remaining crab and noodles. Arrange the coriander leaves on top, pushing them down lightly. Finally, pour over the filling mixture. Bake for 1-1$^1/_2$ hours, until a fine knife tip inserted into the centre comes out clean. Slide the quiche on to a wire rack and lift off the flan ring.

Beef, Wild Mushroom and Claret Pie

DIANA HENRY

Serves 6

30g dried wild mushrooms
2 tablespoons groundnut oil
1kg braising beef, cut in 2cm cubes
350g shallots
50g butter
1 stick celery, finely chopped
2 cloves garlic, crushed
30g plain flour
300ml claret
Leaves from 3 sprigs fresh thyme
3 bay leaves
300g fresh mushrooms, cleaned and sliced
3 tablespoons finely chopped parsley
450g puff pastry for one big pie, or 600g for
    6 small pies
1 beaten egg
Salt and freshly ground black pepper

Pour enough boiling water over the dried mushrooms to cover and leave to soak. In a heavy casserole heat 2 tablespoons of oil and brown the meat well on all sides. (Do this in batches so that the temperature remains high to fry the meat rather than sweat it.) Remove and set aside. If you haven't burnt the oil, add the peeled shallots to the pan and lightly brown them on the outside. If the oil is burnt, use fresh in a clean pan. Turn the heat down, add 20g of the butter and sweat the celery and garlic with the shallots for about 5 minutes.

Return the meat, with any juices, to the casserole. Season well and, on a low heat, add the flour and stir everything round until well coated. Cut up any large soaked mushrooms, then add all of them to the casserole with their soaking liquid. Add the claret, thyme and bay leaves and bring to the boil. Immediately turn down the heat, cover, and cook on a very gentle heat for 1½ hours, stirring every so often, and taking the cover off the pan for the last 15 minutes to reduce the liquid.

Melt the remaining butter in a sauté pan and cook the fresh mushrooms over a fairly high heat so that they become well coloured. Season and cook until they exude their liquid and the liquid evaporates (if any liquid remains in the mushrooms or the pan, it may make the gravy watery). Let the mixture cool.

Stir the mushrooms and parsley into the casserole and check the seasoning. Put the meat in one large or six small pie dishes. Roll out the pastry. Cut a strip, or strips, large enough to go around the edge of the pie dish or dishes. Brush the edge of the dish with water and press the pastry strip on to it; dampen this with water and then cover with the pastry, pressing it down on to the pastry strip. Trim off the excess pastry, knock up the edges and then crimp round the pie. Use remaining pastry to decorate. Brush well with beaten egg and then chill for half an hour. Bake in an oven heated to 220°C, Gas 7 for 35-40 minutes for one large pie, or 25-30 minutes for smaller pies. Serve immediately.

Chicken, Leek and Morel Pie

TOM PARKER BOWLES

I got this recipe from Gary Robinson, who is a wonderful chef. I've cooked it a number of times and it is exquisite.

Serves 6

20g dried morel mushrooms
6 free range organic skinless boneless chicken
    fillets, about 750g
10 baby leeks, trimmed and washed
30g butter
15g flour
300ml double cream
Leaves from 2 large sprigs fresh tarragon
Squeeze fresh lemon juice
About 300g shortcrust pastry ($^2/_3$ x 500g pack)
1 free range egg yolk, plus 1 teaspoon water
Sea salt and freshly ground black pepper

Soak the morels in about 750ml just boiled water for 10 minutes until softened. Strain, reserving the liquid. Slice the mushrooms.

Cut the chicken into chunks about 2cm dice. Slice the baby leeks thinly. Put the reserved liquid into a large pan and bring to the boil. Stir in the morels, leeks, chicken and seasoning. Return to a gentle boil, stirring then cover and poach on a very gentle heat for about 15 minutes when the meat will be just cooked and tender.

Strain off the liquid, and set aside 300ml. (Don't waste the remainder it will be great for soup or a casserole.)

Heat the butter in the same pan and when hot stir in the chicken, morels and leek. Then sprinkle over the flour and mix in and cook over a very low heat for a couple of minutes until it browns a little.

Gradually mix in the 300ml stock until smooth and then the cream. Bring to a simmer, stirring. Meanwhile, chop the tarragon and mix in along with seasoning and a squeeze of lemon juice for flavour. Remove and cool. The filling can be chilled at this point.

Make the pastry top. Choose a pie dish about 1.5 litre capacity. Roll out the pastry to a 3mm thickness (like a £1 coin). Use the top as a template and cut out a shape about 5mm larger than the dish top. Spoon the filling into the pie dish and lift over the pastry top pressing down around the edge lightly. Make a slit in the centre and brush with the egg yolk glaze. Trimmings can be cut into leaves as a decoration.

Set the pie aside whilst you heat the oven to 180ºC, Gas 4. Then bake the pie (placed on a shallow roasting pan) for 30-40 minutes until it is golden brown and crisp.

Fig and Nutella Pastries

ALASTAIR HENDY

In the fresh fig season, try these delectable and chic little tarts made quick and easy by using Jus-Rol pastry, sandwiched with a filling of Nutella and topped with gorgeous glazed figs. If you don't want to make your own glaze use warmed runny apricot jam instead - and dollop on that cream thick and fast on serving. Guaranteed yum!

Serves 4

10 large ripe purple figs, thickly sliced lengthways
1 x 425g pack Jus-Rol ready rolled puff pastry, thawed if frozen
4 tablespoons Nutella hazelnut chocolate spread
1 small egg, lightly beaten
4 heaped tablespoons golden caster sugar
Whipped double cream or crème fraîche, to serve
A little ground cinnamon, optional

Preheat the oven to 200° C, Gas 6. Unroll the pastry onto a lightly floured surface, then stamp out 8 discs – each a little more in diameter than the combined height of 2 figs, about 10-12 cm diameter. Place four of the discs on a greased non-stick baking sheet or one lined with a sheet of baking paper. Spread each of these thickly with the Nutella, leaving a 1cm border clear of spread, then brush the border with beaten egg and carefully lay the other discs on top and seal the edges only without pressing down where the chocolate sits.

Snip the tops from the figs and thickly slice each fig lengthways. Reserve the end slices of figs for the glaze and lay the whole slices in an overlapping spiral around each pastry leaving a 1cm border. Brush this border with more beaten egg, sprinkle the fruit with half of the sugar and bake on the top shelf of the oven for about 20 minutes or until puffed up and golden. Remove to a wire rack and cool.

Meanwhile, throw the end slices of fig into a pan with the remaining sugar and 100ml of water and bring to a fast bubble. Cook until you have a sticky yet syrupy jam, stirring occasionally, then strain into a bowl.

As the pastries cool, brush all over with the warm jam and serve freshly baked with cream or crème fraîche which can be dusted with pinches of cinnamon.

Pumpkin and Almond Tart

ALBERT ROUX

This divine Provençal tart is traditionally served at Christmas in France. It is a very old recipe, which is nowadays found only in the remoter parts of the region.

Serves 8

300g wedge pumpkin
120g whole blanched almonds
120g golden caster sugar
30g dried orange zests or grated zest of 2 fresh oranges
$1/2$ teaspoon orange flower water (optional)
A little flour, to dust
300g puff pastry, thawed if frozen ($2/3$ x 500g pack)
1 egg yolk beaten with one tablespoon milk
A little golden granulated sugar, to serve (optional)

To prepare the pumpkin, using a sharp knife, cut off the skin and seeds, then chop the flesh into small 1cm pieces and place in a saucepan with 3 tablespoons water. Cover the pan and cook over a low heat, stirring occasionally with a wooden spatula until you can crush the softened pumpkin with the spatula, about 10-15 minutes. Purée the pumpkin in a food processor or blender, return it to the pan and cook over a low heat stirring continuously, until thick and smooth, about 10 minutes. Transfer the purée to a bowl and cool.

Toast the almonds under a hot grill until pale golden. Take care not to burn them as they colour quickly. Put in the food processor with the sugar and the orange zests and grind into small pieces. Stir these into the pumpkin purée and add the orange flower water if you are using it.

Cut off 50g of pastry and reserve. Roll out the remaining pastry on a lightly floured marble or wooden surface into a 25cm circle, 2-3 mm thick (like a £1 coin). Brush a non-stick baking sheet with water and lay the pastry on the sheet. Brush the border with egg wash, roll it over and pinch up the edge to make a small rim to hold the filling.

Spoon the pumpkin and almond filling into the centre and using a palette knife, spread it evenly over the pastry. Brush the outer rim of the pastry with egg wash. Roll the remaining pastry into a long rectangle and cut into 1cm strips. Arrange these on top of the tart as a lattice forming a criss-cross pattern. Brush with the rest of the egg wash. Chill in fridge for 20 minutes whilst you preheat oven to 200°C, Gas 6. Bake the tart in the preheated oven for 35 minutes until risen and golden, then immediately slide it onto a wire rack to cool completely.

Sprinkle the tart with a little granulated sugar, if you like, and serve it whole on a round china plate.

Chocolate Truffle Tartlets

ANGELA HARTNETT

These make dainty little rich chocolate mouthfuls, to be served as petits fours.

Makes 24

1 x 340g pack sweet dessert pastry, thawed if
    frozen

Filling
24 large seedless raisins
1 tablespoon dark rum or brandy
125ml double cream
5 tablespoons milk
125g dark chocolate of 70% cocoa solids, e.g.
    Valrhona Guanaja
24 fresh raspberries or small walnut halves
    or 12 of each

Put the raisins and rum into a small pan and heat until the rum or brandy starts to sizzle. Remove and cool so the alcohol seeps into the raisins.

Roll out the pastry to a 3mm thickness (like a £1 coin) and cut out 24 x 6cm rounds. (The pastry is quite soft, so either work with it straight from the fridge, or roll between two large sheets of cling film.) Line these into 2 x 12 hole small tartlet or bun tins. Prick the bases and set aside for 20 minutes whilst you preheat the oven to 200°C, Gas 6. Bake the tart cases blind for 10-12 minutes (see page 9), pricking the bases if they rise. Cool on a wire tray until crisp.

Meanwhile, boil half the cream and all the milk in a small pan. Break up the chocolate and place in a heatproof bowl. Pour over the boiling cream and stir in one direction only to make sure the chocolate is well melted and smooth. Cool to room temperature. Whip the remaining cream and fold into the chocolate. Spoon the chocolate into a piping bag fitted with a small star or plain nozzle. Put a soaked raisin into the centre of each tart case and pipe over the chocolate in tiny dabs. Top each little tart with a walnut half or raspberry or both. Serve at room temperature so the filling remains creamy.

Apple Parcels with Calvados Butter Sauce

ANTON EDELMANN

It is culturally and socially necessary to teach our children to cook, otherwise the world will be a poorer place in the future.

Makes 4

60g sultanas
1¹/₂ tablespoons Calvados
A good pinch of ground cinnamon
4 Reinette or large Granny Smith apples
300g puff pastry, thawed if frozen (²/₃ x 500g pack)
1 egg yolk, beaten
50g golden caster sugar
2 teaspoons liquid glucose
50g unsalted butter
125ml double cream
25g icing sugar

Mix the sultanas with the Calvados for an hour then drain, reserving the Calvados. Sprinkle the sultanas with the cinnamon. Preheat the oven to 190°C, Gas 5.

Core the apples making holes of at least about 1.5cm, then top and tail them with a sharp knife so that they stand level.

Roll out the puff pastry on a lightly floured board to a rectangle 36 x 25cm about 3mm thickness (like a £1 coin) then cut into four smaller rectangles about 18 x 12.5cm each. Stand an apple in the centre of each piece of pastry and press the sultanas into the cavity of the apples using the end of a teaspoon if necessary.

Brush the edges of the rectangles with the beaten egg yolk. Wrap each rectangle up and around an apple and place on a baking sheet. Make a small cut in the top of each apple parcel then brush with the remaining egg glaze. Bake the apple parcels for 20 minutes until golden and crisp.

Meanwhile, place the caster sugar, with 3 tablespoons of water and the liquid glucose in a heavy-based pan. Heat up the mixture, stirring until it dissolves and cook briskly until the syrup turns to a pale amber colour. Remove from the heat and stir in the butter and 125ml of the double cream until melted then mix in the reserved Calvados and pour it through a fine-meshed sieve.

After the apple parcels have been baking for 20 minutes remove them from the oven and dust generously with the icing sugar.

Serve each apple parcel on a warm serving plate and pour around the butter sauce.

Pineapple and Black Pepper Tarte Tatin

CURTIS STONE

I am delighted to contribute this recipe to such a good cause. It is a restaurant-style recipe usually cooked to order. I have adapted it to feed four people for a dinner party. If you have only one pan, then keep the first tatin warm whilst you make the second.

Makes 2 tarts, each serves 2

120g unsalted butter
120g golden caster sugar
10cm thick slice fresh pineapple, cored
1 teaspoon coarsely ground black pepper
1 x 212g sheet ready rolled puff pastry, thawed
    if frozen (half a 425g pack)
Good quality vanilla ice cream, to serve

Press the butter over the base of 2 small blini or cast iron pans approximately 10cm in diameter and at least 5cm deep. Sprinkle the sugar on top.

Slice the pineapple in two, horizontally and sprinkle one side of each piece with the pepper. Place the pineapple, pepper-side down, onto the sugar.

Cut out 2 x 14cm circles of pastry and place on top of the pineapple so the edges hang over. Tuck these down to fit snugly between the pineapple and the pan sides then allow to rest for 10 minutes. At the same time, preheat the oven to 190°C, Gas 5. Place the pans over a low heat on top of the stove for 3 to 5 minutes until you see the sugar begin to bubble up around the side of the pastry and turn light brown.

Transfer to the oven and bake for 30 minutes until risen, golden brown and crisp. Remove and rest for 10 minutes, then carefully invert each pan onto a plate, taking care that the hot syrup does not run down your hands. Cut each tatin in half and place on dessert plates. Serve with scoops of vanilla ice cream or pouring cream.

Black, Green and Flame Grape Tart

GINA STEER

Serves 6-8

1 x 28cm round ready rolled shortcrust pastry or
    250g shortcrust, thawed if frozen
400g mascarpone cheese
25g golden caster sugar
1 teaspoon vanilla extract
150g low-fat natural yogurt
About 250g mixture black, flame and green
    seedless grapes

Preheat the oven to 200°C, Gas 6, 15 minutes before cooking. If using a ready rolled round of pastry, simply press into a 23cm round loose based flan tin. Otherwise, roll out the pastry to approximately 28cm on a lightly floured board and lift into the flan tin using a rolling pin. Trim and bake blind according to instructions on page 9. Remove and allow to cool until cold.

When ready to serve, blend together the mascarpone, sugar and vanilla extract until soft and creamy, then gradually beat in the yogurt. Spoon into the cooked pastry case and level the top. Cut the grapes in half and arrange on top before serving.

Custard Tarts

GRACE HENDERSON

I fit squares of pastry into round bun tins for an attractive four-pointed shape.

Makes 8

1 x 340g pack sweet dessert pastry, thawed if frozen
2 large eggs
25g golden caster sugar
A few drops vanilla essence
150ml milk
$\frac{1}{2}$ teaspoon freshly-grated nutmeg

Preheat oven to 200°C, Gas 6. Roll out the pastry thinly and cut out eight 10cm squares, re-rolling the pastry as necessary. Use the squares to line 8 holes of a deep 12-hole muffin tin – the tips look attractive if allowed to poke upwards. Bake in preheated oven for 10 minutes then remove from the oven and whilst still warm, use a piece of kitchen paper to squash the pastry in each case to flatten it. Reduce the oven temperature to 180°C, Gas 4. Beat together the eggs, sugar and vanilla essence. Heat the milk until almost boiling, then stir briskly into the eggs. Strain into a jug and pour into the pastry cases. Grate the nutmeg over the tops, then bake for 15-20 minutes or until the custard has set. Leave to cool then carefully remove from the tin.

Yorkshire Curd Tart

JAMES MARTIN

Serve this deliciously simple great British classic with a selection of summer berries which can be lightly stewed to a compôte if liked. By baking the pastry case blind untrimmed, then trimming it after baking, you ensure the pastry case doesn't shrink back. It's a clever chef's trick.

Serves 8-12

1 x 340g sweet dessert pastry, thawed if frozen
500ml whipping cream
8 free range egg yolks
75g golden caster sugar
$\frac{1}{2}$ teaspoon ground allspice (or 1 teaspoon allspice berries, crushed in a pestle and mortar)

Roll out the pastry on a lightly floured work surface and, using a rolling pin, lift into a 27cm lightly buttered flan dish leaving any excess pastry hanging over the edge until after it is cooked. Prick the base.

Line with baking parchment paper and fill with rice or baking beans, then chill for 20-30 minutes whilst you heat the oven to 180°C, Gas 4.

Bake in the oven for 15 minutes. Once the pastry shell is cooked, remove from the oven and take the greaseproof paper and rice or baking beans out. Cool for 5 minutes then using a sharp knife, neatly trim the top edge. Turn the oven down to 130°C, Gas 1.

Make the filling. Heat the cream in a pan until on the point of boiling. In a heatproof bowl, beat together the egg yolks with the caster sugar and half the allspice. Pour the hot cream onto the mixture, whisking well (take care not to let the egg yolks curdle) and then pour through a sieve into a jug. Pour this mixture into the cooked pastry case.

Sprinkle with the remaining allspice and bake in the oven for 35-45 minutes until the custard is just set. It might still be slightly runny in the centre, but this will set on cooling. Do not overcook or the filling will go too hard.

Remove from the oven and cool to room temperature and serve cut into slices with summer berries alongside.

Chocolate Tart with Orange Scented English Cream

JOHN WILLIAMS

I am delighted that Jus-Rol has chosen to support the Adopt a School Trust as part of its 50th Anniversary celebrations. By providing chefs to primary and secondary schools to teach children about the pleasure, variety and provenance of food and how to cook, the charity is doing a tremendous job in getting children interested in all aspects of food from an early age – and the more funding we get the more we are able to continue this much needed work.

Makes 1 tart to serve 6

340g pack sweet dessert pastry, thawed if frozen
Ganache filling
330g dark chocolate, about 60% cocoa solids
2 medium free range eggs
130ml milk
230ml double cream
Orange Scented English Cream
125ml milk
125ml cream
Zest of 1 orange
1 vanilla pod, seeds scraped out
4 egg yolks
45g golden caster sugar

Roll out the pastry to a 4mm thickness and line a 23-24cm tart tin (2cm depth) with a removable base, making sure the edges extend up slightly about the rim. Prick the base.

Heat the oven to 170ºC, Gas 3. Bake blind (see page 9) for about 45 minutes until pale golden and crisp. Remove the baking paper and beans.

Meanwhile, make the filling. Chop or break the chocolate into small pieces and place in a heatproof bowl.

Whisk the eggs in another heatproof bowl. Bring the milk and cream just to the boil then pour onto the eggs, whisking as you pour.

Return the mixture to the pan and on the lowest heat possible, stir gently until the mixture begins to thicken slightly to a light custard. Don't overheat or it will curdle.

Pour this mixture through a fine sieve onto the chopped chocolate and stir until it melts. Pour through a sieve into the cooked tartlet base and set aside to cool. You may not need all the chocolate custard, it depends on the depth of your tart tin but try and get the chocolate as high as possible. Allow to cool and lightly set. Do not chill, the filling should be at room temperature.

Whilst it is setting, make the orange cream. Beat together the 125ml milk and cream, zest of orange and vanilla seeds and bring to the boil. Beat the egg yolks and 45g sugar in a heatproof bowl until thick and creamy then slowly pour the just boiled creamy milk onto the mixture, whisking well. Return to a very gentle heat and stir until the mixture thickens slightly and coats the back of a spoon. Remove immediately so it doesn't overheat. Cool, then cut the tart in slices and serve with the cream.

Apple and Prune Tarts

ROWLEY LEIGH

This can be made in one large tart case, using a sweet pastry, but individual ones are lighter and more crisp.

Makes 6

A mug of hot black tea
18 prunes
1 large Bramley apple
1 clove
Some freshly grated nutmeg
6 Russet apples
About 2 tablespoons lemon juice
25g butter
250g puff pastry, thawed if frozen
4 egg yolks
2 teaspoons milk
1 tablespoon Calvados or cider brandy or rum
50g golden caster sugar, plus 2-3 teaspoons for cooking the apples
50g unsalted butter, melted

Pour hot tea over the prunes and simmer gently for five minutes before leaving to swell for half an hour, then drain (reserving a little tea), halve and stone them (if needed). Peel and core the Bramley, chop it into small pieces and put in a pan with a dessertspoon of water, a teaspoon of sugar, a clove and a pinch of nutmeg. Cook it gently until softened, stirring to make a smooth purée. Leave to cool whilst you preheat the oven to 220°C, Gas 7.

Peel the Russets, cut each into 6 segments and cut out the cores. Toss the apples in a little lemon juice and then fry them in hot butter with a teaspoon or two of sugar added. This needs to be a very hot flame as you should aim to colour the apples without cooking them. Drain them quickly and reserve.

Roll the pastry out thinly, cut into 6 discs of 14cm diameter and place them on a baking tray lined with a sheet of baking parchment. Spoon the purée onto the rounds, leaving a good 1cm border. Arrange alternating pieces of Russet and prune in a circle on top of the purée, still leaving a border.

Beat 1 egg yolk with the milk for a glaze. Brush the border with the glaze and bake these tarts for 15 minutes.

Meanwhile beat the remaining 3 yolks with a teaspoon of the prune flavoured tea, the alcohol and the 50g sugar. Using an electric whisk, beat this to a sabayon (i.e. white and frothy foam) before pouring in the melted butter in a thin stream, whisking as you do so. Spoon this over the fruit in the tarts and return to the oven for six minutes until it sets lightly and browns.

Serve hot or cold, with cream or ice cream.

Layered Toffee Apple Pastry

LESLEY WATERS

I think it is very important to get children into the kitchen and cooking at an early age. If you are trying out this recipe, why not get them to brush butter over the filo and help core and slice the apple. This is a recipe I dreamed up quickly for a Ready, Steady Cook show and found it ideal for the whole family.

Serves 2

120g unsalted butter
3 sheets of filo pastry, 50 x 24cm thawed
3 Cox's apples, cored and sliced
120ml double cream
120g unrefined soft brown sugar
About 1 tablespoon icing sugar, to dust

Preheat the oven to 220°C, Gas 7. Line a baking sheet with baking parchment. Melt the butter in a medium pan. Cut the filo sheets into 12 x 12cm squares and make them into 4 piles, brushing with half the butter in between. Place on the baking sheet and bake in the oven for 4-5 minutes, until crisp and golden. Remove from the oven onto a wire rack and cool.

Sauté the sliced apple for about 3-4 minutes in the remaining melted butter until golden and lightly softened. Add the cream and sugar to the pan and simmer gently for 3-4 minutes.

Lay two of the filo squares on dessert plates, spoon over the apple mixture, top with remaining filo and dust with icing sugar. Trickle any leftover sauce around and serve.

Summer Fruit Tarts

LUCY KNOX AND KEITH RICHMOND

The earlier you can get children involved in cooking the better. And it needs to be fun - cooking shouldn't sound like a chore that ends with washing up. If young people can understand about food, where it comes from and how ingredients can be 'magicked' into delicious dishes it will help them in the future. The more you understand and appreciate food, the more likely you are to enjoy a healthy diet and a more productive life. These tarts are delicious and also look wonderful – they are a great thing to make if you feel like surprising and showing off in front of your friends. Easy to make and a real treat.

Serves 6

250g shortcrust pastry, thawed if frozen
125g white chocolate, broken into pieces
250g mascarpone
1 tablespoon Cointreau, optional
142ml carton double cream
200g mixed red berries, sliced strawberries and
    raspberries etc
Fresh basil, to serve

Preheat the oven to 180ºC, Gas 4. Roll out the pastry to 3mm (the thickness of a £1 coin) and cut out six rounds about 14cm diameter, re-rolling if necessary.

Use to line 6 x 10cm tartlet tins, pressing well into the sides and trimming tops leaving a little standing above the rim. Put them on a baking sheet, prick the bases with a fork and line with baking parchment and dried beans. Bake blind (see page 9) for 10 minutes, remove the paper and beans and bake for a further 5 minutes or until golden brown. Leave to cool completely.

Meanwhile, make the filling. Put the chocolate and mascarpone in a bowl and place over a pan of barely simmering water until the chocolate has melted. (Alternatively, this can be done in a microwave on a defrost setting for about 2-3 minutes.) Do not let the chocolate overheat or it will 'seize'. Add the Cointreau if using, stir to combine and leave to cool to room temperature. Whip the cream until it forms soft peaks, then stir into the cooled chocolate mixture. Pour into the cooled tart cases (you may have some left over) and chill for about an hour until lightly set. Top with berries and dainty basil leaves then serve. Don't over chill the filling – it should be deliciously creamy.

Treacle and Coconut Tart

MARCUS WAREING

I suggest you make the filling a day ahead and let it stand in the fridge.

Makes 23cm tart to serve 6-8

225g golden syrup
60g fresh white breadcrumbs
40g desiccated coconut
1 free range medium egg, beaten
100ml double cream
1 x 340g sweet dessert pastry, thawed if frozen
About 3 tablespoons jam – raspberry or apricot,
    slightly warmed until runny
120g fresh blueberries, optional
A little sifted icing sugar, to dust

Stand the tin of golden syrup in a pan of just boiled water for about 5 minutes to soften it a little. Place a mixing bowl on the scales and pour in the runny syrup to the required weight. Beat in the breadcrumbs, coconut, beaten egg and cream. Ideally chill for 24 hours because it makes a lighter filling.

Roll out the pastry on a lightly floured board to a 5mm thickness, approximately 30cm diameter and lift into a 23cm loose bottomed flan tin, about 1.5cm deep, using the rolling pin to transfer the pastry. If it cracks, simply pinch it together. Press the pastry well into the sides and trim the top. Leave to rest for 20 minutes in the fridge whilst you heat the oven to 190°C, Gas 5.

Warm the jam a little if necessary and spread in the flan base using the back of a spoon. Scoop the filling on top; it should come three quarters the way up the flan. If using, drop in the blueberries so they are resting on top.

Bake for about 30 minutes until the filling is risen and golden brown. Allow the tart to cool to room temperature before serving dusted with a little sifted icing sugar.

Frangipane Mince Pies

MARGUERITE PATTEN OBE

In Praise of Pastry: Generations of children and adults have delighted in the taste and texture of good pastry. As children discover the pleasure of learning to cook well they will find that pastry is a perfect partner to a wide range of healthy savoury and sweet ingredients.

Makes 12

250g shortcrust pastry, thawed if frozen
$^1/_2$ x 400g jar luxury quality mincemeat
Frangipane
25g butter, melted
50g golden caster sugar
50g ground almonds
A few drops almond extract
1 medium egg, beaten
Topping
25g flaked almonds
About 24 dried cranberries, optional
A little sifted icing sugar, to dust

Roll out the pastry to about 3mm (the thickness of a £1 coin) on a lightly floured worktop. Using a 7.5cm fluted pastry cutter stamp out 12 rounds. Press these into deep patty tins and chill for around 20 minutes whilst you preheat the oven to 200°C, Gas 6.

Place a teaspoonful of mincemeat into the bottom of each pastry case. Mix together all the ingredients for the frangipane and carefully spread over the mincemeat. Press the flaked almonds on top of the soft mixture and add cranberries, if liked.

Bake for 18 to 20 minutes, or until the pastry is golden and the filling firm. Cool in the tins for 5 minutes then turn out onto a wire rack and cool completely. Serve freshly baked dusted with some icing sugar, if liked.

Berry and White Chocolate Tarts

WILLIAM SITWELL

Quick, easy and very scrummy! Children can help to roll out the pastry and stamp out the circles. Then you could introduce them to the delights of hulling fresh strawberries and brushing over the jelly glaze.

Serves 6

1 x 340g pack sweet dessert pastry
6 tablespoons mascarpone
400g medium size strawberries, hulled and sliced
100g fresh raspberries
3-4 tablespoons redcurrant jelly, melted

Roll out the pastry on a lightly floured surface and cut into six 12cm circles re-rolling the pastry trimmings as necessary. Don't worry if the pastry cracks a little, simply pinch it together. Place on a non-stick baking sheet and prick with a fork. Chill for 5 minutes whilst you preheat the oven to 200°C, Gas 6. Then bake for 10-15 minutes or until golden brown and crisp. Cool on a wire rack.

Spread a tablespoon of mascarpone on each disc, then arrange the strawberries in a circle on top. Pile the raspberries in the middle. Heat the redcurrant jelly in a small pan stirring until melted and smooth. Brush over the fruits and allow to cool for a few minutes. Serve as soon as possible.

Strawberry Mille Feuille with Vanilla Diplomat Crème

CLAIRE CLARK

Serves 8

1 x 425g pack ready rolled puff pastry, thawed
   if frozen
40g each of plain flour and cornflour
500ml milk
5 egg yolks
100g golden caster sugar
1 vanilla pod
250ml double cream
4-6 good quality strawberry jam, sieved
400g strawberries, small and even sized
2 tablespoons icing sugar

Heat the oven to 200°C, Gas 6. Line a large baking sheet with baking parchment and lay the pastry sheets on top. Prick well with a fork, cover with another sheet of baking parchment and top with a second metal sheet. (If the baking sheets are too small then bake the pastry singly.) Bake for about 20-25 minutes. Remove tray and paper and check to see if the pastry is golden brown and crisp; if not return to the oven for another 5 minutes or so. Cool on a wire rack.

Meanwhile make the crème. Sift together the two flours and set aside. Put the milk onto boil. Whilst it is heating, slit the vanilla pod in half lengthways and add to the pan. In a large heatproof bowl, beat the egg yolks and sugar until smooth. Add the sifted flours into this mix and cream to a smooth paste. When the milk has boiled, remove the vanilla pod, allow to cool a little, then scrape out the seeds with a knife tip and add to the milk. Discard the pod. Gradually pour the hot milk onto the egg mixing well until smooth. Return this mix to a clean pan and over a medium heat bring back to the boil whisking continuously and simmer for a further minute. Remove from the heat and pour the pastry crème into a bowl. Cover with cling film and cool.

Whisk double cream until stiff. Then whisk cold pastry crème until smooth and fold the two mixtures together with a large metal spoon. Spoon half into a piping bag fitted with a 1cm plain nozzle. Hull, wash and dry the strawberries.

Using a large serrated knife, cut pastry widthways into three, for six equal rectangles. Spread strawberry jam on two pastry rectangles and top with two more, like sandwiches. Divide most of the remaining cream on top of each sandwich and spread neatly to the edges. Press the strawberries in neat rows into the cream. Pipe the reserved cream in between the fruits and around the edges so they are completely covered. Then top with the final two rectangles, pressing down lightly, and smooth the edges with a palette knife. Chill in the fridge for at least 30 minutes until the filling firms. To serve, cut each mille feuille into four using the sharp knife again. Dust with icing sugar.

Plum and Ginger
Melt in the Mouth Tart

VANESSA FELTZ AND NIGEL BARDEN

For a chic French-style tart, use a long tart tin with a removable base, otherwise a Swiss roll tin will be fine, but line it with a long strip of baking parchment that overhangs the edges so it can be carefully lifted out to serve. The tart truly does live up to its name!

Serves 4

1 x 270g pack Jus-Rol filo pastry (six 50 x 24cm sheets), thawed
About 40-50g butter, melted
3 tablespoons ginger jam
10 small sweet red plums (Kirke's Blue, Czar, or less if larger variety, such as Victoria)
1 dessertspoon golden caster sugar, optional

Preheat the oven to 180°C, Gas 4. Using a long tart tin with a removable base of 36 x 12cm (or a Swiss roll tin) brush lightly with a little of the melted butter. (If the tin has a fixed base then lay a long strip of baking parchment the width of the tin inside with edges overhanging so you can lift it out to serve.)

Lay a sheet of filo in the tin and brush it lightly with more butter, pressing the sheet well into the sides. Repeat with the other 6 sheets, then trim the edges with scissors leaving an overhanging edge of about 2cm. Don't butter the last sheet. Instead, melt the ginger jam with a tablespoon of water on a low heat and brush this on in its place.

Cut the plums into quarters, remove the stones, place in rows pressing them up against each other.

If the plums are a little sharp, or you have a particularly sweet tooth, sprinkle over the spoon of sugar.

Bake for 12-15 minutes until pastry is just crispy on the edges and the plums are caramelising nicely. Cool until warm then remove from the tin to a board and serve cut in thick slices. Serve with a little trickle of half fat crème fraîche or try a low fat lemon yogurt.

Cinnamon Fruit Cigars

MARK HIX

As the father of twin daughters, Mark is a firm believer in getting children into the kitchen and regularly gives demonstrations to young cooks pulling them up on stage to get them stirring and chopping. He has also written a popular children's cookbook, called *Eat Up*.

Makes about 8-10

150g dates, stoned
100g dried apricots, stoned
50g raisins
30g nibbed or chopped almonds
30g unsalted pistachios, chopped
1 teaspoon ground cinnamon
40g butter, melted
1 teaspoon icing sugar
2 teaspoons ground cinnamon
5-6 sheets of filo pastry, 50 x 24cm

Soak the dates, apricots and raisins in warm water overnight. Drain the fruit, pat dry with paper towel and chop it quite finely with a heavy knife, but don't be tempted to put it into a food processor as you may end up with a purée on your hands that won't bind in the filo pastry and will simply be a mess. Mix the fruit with the nuts and half the cinnamon.

Cut the filo sheets into 10 x 15cm squares then cover with cling film so they don't dry out.

Preheat the oven to 200°C, Gas 6. Lay a sheet of filo on a flat surface and put a couple of heaped teaspoons along the edge of the pastry nearest to you, spreading it into a strip, leaving about 1cm at either side. Fold these ends over to form a hem down each side, then brush all the pastry right to the edges with melted butter. Now roll the pastry up as tightly as you can into a cigar shape and put onto a greased non-stick baking tray (or one lined with a sheet of baking parchment) with the join facing down. Repeat with the other sheets of pastry and the rest of the mixture.

Space the cigars out, leaving 3-4 cm between them on the tray, then brush them with the remaining melted butter.

Bake for about 10-12 minutes until golden, then leave to cool on the tray for about 5-10 minutes for the cigars to crisp a little. Put the icing sugar and remaining cinnamon into a fine-meshed sieve and dust the cigars by tapping the rim of the sieve against your hand over the cigars. Serve warm, with thick cream or yogurt to dip them into.

Lemon Tart with Chocolate and Honey Ice Cream

SARA JAYNE STANES

I am the director of The Academy of Culinary Arts and am responsible for the Adopt a School Trust charity so I am naturally delighted that Jus-Rol has put together this exciting recipe book to support us. These two recipes make an unusual but perfect partnership.

Makes one 25cm tart

500g Jus-Rol shortcrust pastry, thawed
4 large lemons
275ml double cream
450g golden caster sugar
9 eggs

Roll out the pastry on a lightly floured table top to the thickness of a £1 coin and line into a 25cm flan ring. Rest the tart in the fridge for 30 minutes then line with baking parchment or foil and baking beans and bake 'blind' at 180°C, Gas 4 (see page 9) for 20 minutes. Remove the baking beans and paper or foil and return to the oven for another 5-10 minutes until the pastry is golden brown and cooked. Remove and cool. Reduce the oven temperature to 140°C, Gas 1.

Meanwhile, make the filling. Grate the zest from the lemons and squeeze the juice.

In a large bowl, whisk together the cream and sugar and add the eggs, one at a time, and then the lemon juice. Pour the mixture through a fine sieve and then mix in the zest.

Pour into the baked flan case and bake for a further 45-60 minutes until lightly set. It sets further as it cools. Serve in wedges with scoops of chocolate and honey ice cream, opposite.

Chocolate and Honey Ice Cream

Makes about 750ml

150g dark chocolate 70% cocoa solids, finely
    chopped
425ml double cream
50g clear honey
25g golden caster sugar
3 egg yolks

Finely chop the chocolate using a heavy bladed knife. Boil 100ml of the cream. Remove from the heat and stir in the chocolate until smooth.

Beat the honey with the caster sugar in a large heatproof bowl using a whisk then beat in the egg yolks.

Bring the remaining cream to the boil then pour on to the sugar and egg yolk mix whisking well to blend. Return the mix to a clean pan and cook over a very low heat stirring all the time. Do not boil; cook until the mix just coats the back of a spoon then pour through a sieve into another bowl. Mix with the chocolate and cream mixture until smooth.

Cool and chill before churning in an ice cream machine until solid. Scoop into an ice cream container to freeze. Allow to thaw for 10 minutes before serving in scoops.

Index